THE MAYA

Jerome Martin

Illustrated by Adam Larkum

Designed by Alice Reese and Poppy Pearce

Maya consultant: Lucia R. Henderson, PhD,
Specialist in Pre-Columbian Art History
Reading consultant: Alison Kelly

Contents

Jungles and volcanoes

The Maya are people who have lived in Mexico and Central America for thousands of years.

Long ago, they built their homes in jungles and in valleys between steep volcanoes.

The jungles were full of animals such as monkeys and jaguars.

Stone cities

This is what a Maya city might have looked like around 1,500 years ago.

Nobles and rulers lived in palaces.

Markets were held in open spaces called plazas.

Most people lived in huts with grass roofs.

Maya temples

Special courts were built for playing a ball game.

The players hit a rubber ball to and fro using only their hips and thighs.

5

Towering temples

Maya temples were built to look like the steep mountains where their gods lived.

This ancient temple is in the city of Tikal.

It was once brightly painted.

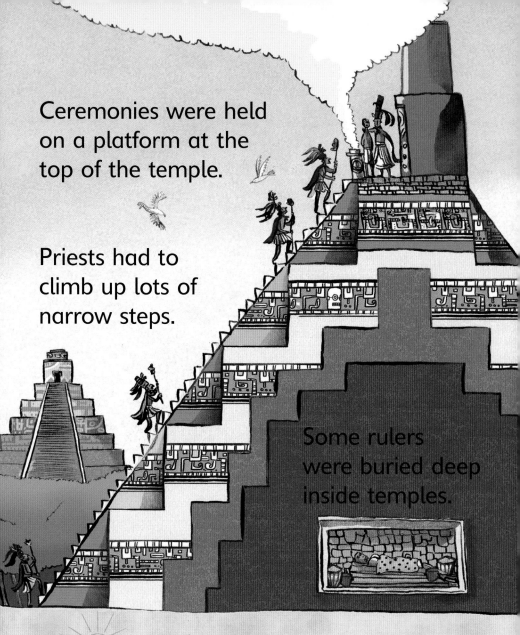

Ceremonies were held
on a platform at the
top of the temple.

Priests had to
climb up lots of
narrow steps.

Some rulers
were buried deep
inside temples.

Temples were often built to
line up with the Sun or stars.

Lords of the Maya

Each Maya city had its own ruler, called the 'ajaw'. He was very powerful and wealthy.

This stone carving shows an ajaw called Shield Jaguar.

He is getting dressed for a battle.

At ceremonies, the ajaw performed special dances to please the gods.

He also had to feed the gods by piercing his body and offering them his blood.

This is Shield Jaguar's wife, Lady Xoc (say 'Shock'). She is bringing him a helmet shaped like a jaguar's head.

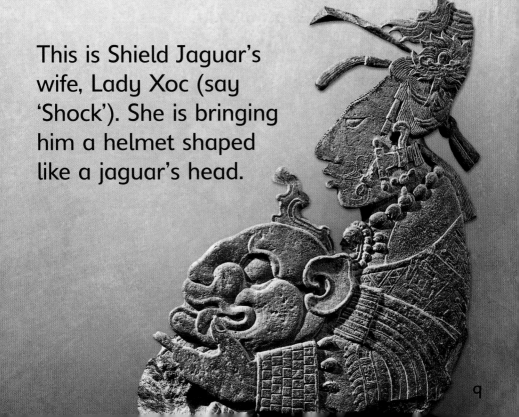

9

Born to rule

Preparing for life as a noble or an ajaw began as soon as a baby was born.

Noble parents squeezed their babies' skulls between two boards. This gave their heads a tall, flat shape that people liked.

This clay figure shows a noble mother with her baby.

Noble children had their ears and lips pierced for ear flares and ornaments.

Boys were sent away to other cities to live with great rulers and learn good manners.

When an ajaw died, his son became the new ajaw and chose a new name for himself.

A few Maya women also became powerful rulers.

Jungle warfare

Maya cities were often at war with one another.

Warriors went into battle wearing costumes and war paint.

They blew trumpets and banged drums to scare their enemies.

They fought with spears and shields and tried to capture enemy warriors.

Some prisoners became slaves. Others were killed during ceremonies.

You can call me "He Who Captured Flaming Jaguar".

Many ajaws added the names of famous prisoners to their own.

13

Roads, ships and trade

Maya traders would travel hundreds of miles to find rare goods and take them to markets to sell.

Their customers liked shells, cloth, feathers, chocolate and precious stones.

This ajaw is admiring a string of beads.

This nobleman is offering it as a gift.

Traders carried goods on their backs
and walked from place to place.

Sometimes cities were connected by long,
straight roads made of stone.

People carved canoes from tree trunks to
transport heavy loads by sea.

Canoes could be twice as long as a modern bus.

What to wear

Clothes meant a lot to the Maya. Fine clothes and ornaments showed how important a person was.

Most women wore loose cotton dresses with bright patterns.

Most men wore a piece of material around their waists.

Both women and men put ornaments in their ears.

Ajaws and noble people wore furs, feathers and jewels.

This Maya ruler is getting dressed for a ceremony.

He is wearing a headdress with long feathers.

His ornaments are made from a green stone called jade.

A spotted jaguar skin hangs from his waist.

Some Maya filed their teeth into points, or decorated them with chips of jade.

Eating and drinking

The Maya were good farmers. They planted beans, squash and lots of corn or maize.

Maya farmers grew their vegetables in large fields dug out of the forest.

They gathered fruits such as papaya and avocado and kept bees for honey.

People caught fish, and hunted deer and pig-like animals called peccaries.

The Maya grew cacao beans and made them into many types of chocolate drinks.

These could be sweet, bitter, or spiced with hot peppers.

This clay pot once held chocolate for drinking.

They often stirred their chocolate or blew bubbles into it to make it frothy.

Reading and writing

Mayan writing was made up of pictures which stood for sounds and words.

The pictures often included animals, objects and human faces.

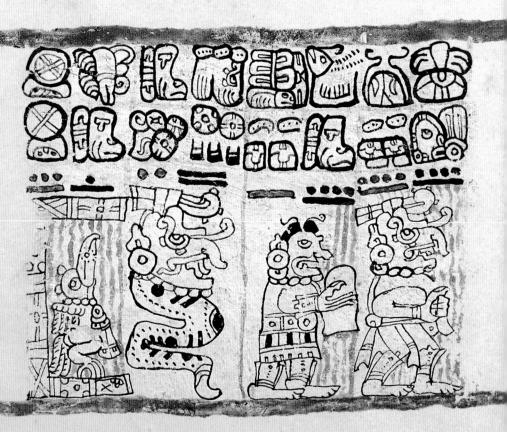

This writing was hard to read. Words could be spelled many different ways.

1. The Maya made paper using the bark from fig trees.

2. They pounded it flat and painted it with white plaster.

3. Scribes wrote on the paper using fine brushes.

4. They folded the paper in a zigzag to make books.

Many scribes kept their brushes in their headdresses.

Nights and days

The Maya studied the night sky carefully.

They learned to predict
how stars and planets
moved across the sky.

They wrote these
movements down in
calendars that measured
days, months and years.

The Maya believed their calendars gave clues to what might happen each day.

Priests said which dates were lucky for holding ceremonies or even battles.

Some dates were so unlucky that people didn't work or even wash themselves.

Some Maya children were named after their birthday.

The Maya gods

The Maya believed in lots of different gods and goddesses. Here are just a few.

The rain god lived in watery caves up in the mountains.

The moon goddess was often shown cuddling a rabbit.

The maize god's head looked like the top of a maize plant.

The wind god was shown playing musical instruments.

This plate shows the god of traders. He carries a heavy pack on his back.

To please the gods, the Maya danced, burned smelly tree sap and offered them gifts of food.

A Maya tale

Maya legends tell of two magical boys, the Hero Twins, who grew up in the forest with their lazy, bullying half-brothers.

The twins had to fetch wood and carry water for their brothers.

They were miserable until one day they came up with a clever trick...

The twins talked their half-brothers into climbing a tree in the forest.

Magically, the tree began to grow.

The bullies were soon stuck on a narrow branch high in the air.

Twist your clothes into tails to balance better!

In a flash, the tails grew hair and the two bullies turned into noisy monkeys.

Spanish invaders

About 500 years ago, people from Spain came to take over the Maya's lands.

Spanish soldiers attacked and captured the Maya's cities, towns and villages.

Many Maya died in the battles, or from illnesses they caught from the Spanish.

The Spanish burned Mayan books and tried to wipe out the Maya's way of life.

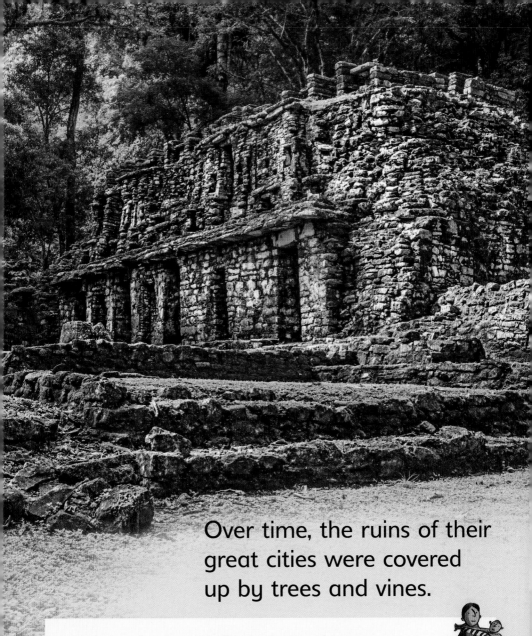

Over time, the ruins of their great cities were covered up by trees and vines.

Although they left their ancient cities, many Maya people still live in Mexico and Central America today.

Glossary

Here are some of the words in this book you might not know. This page tells you what they mean.

 jaguar - a large jungle cat. Its fur has yellow and black spots.

 noble - a rich person. Nobles wore special clothes and precious jewels.

 ajaw - say 'ah-haw'. The ruler of a Maya city.

 ear flare - an ornament that Maya men and women wore in their ears.

headdress - a showy head covering worn by nobles and rulers.

 cacao beans - seeds that can be used to make chocolate.

 scribe - a person whose job it was to write and copy words in books.

Websites to visit

You can visit exciting websites to find out more about the Maya. For links to sites with video clips and activities, go to the Usborne Quicklinks website at **www.usborne.com/quicklinks** and type in the keywords "**beginners maya**".

Always ask an adult before using the internet and make sure you follow these basic rules:
1. Never give out personal information, such as your name, address, school or telephone number.
2. If a website asks you to type in your name or email address, check with an adult first.

The websites are regularly reviewed and the links at Usborne Quicklinks are updated. However, Usborne Publishing is not responsible and does not accept liability for the content or availability of any website other than its own. We recommend that children are supervised while on the internet.

This statue shows a Maya ball game player. He is wearing a large belt to protect his body from the hard rubber ball.

Index

Acknowledgements

Photographic manipulation by John Russell

Additional design by Katie Webb

Photo credits

The publishers are grateful to the following for permission to reproduce material:
Cover © Kenneth Garrett/Danita Delimont/Alamy Stock Photo; **p1** © travelstock.ca/Alamy Stock Photo;
p6 © age fotostock/Alamy Stock Photo; **p8-9** © De Agostini Picture Library/G. Dagli Orti/Bridgeman
Images; **p10** © Justin Kerr, Mayavase.com; **p14** © Justin Kerr, Mayavase.com; **p17** © De Agostini Picture
Library/G. Dagli Orti/Bridgeman Images; **p19** © Museo de Arqueologia, Guatemala/Jean-Pierre Courau/
Bridgeman Images; **p20** © Museo de America, Madrid, Spain/Bridgeman Images; **p25** © Justin Kerr,
Mayavase.com; **p29** © Kelly Cheng/Getty Images; **p31** © World History Archive/Alamy Stock Photo.

Every effort has been made to trace and acknowledge ownership of copyright. If any rights have
been omitted, the publishers offer to rectify this in any subsequent editions following notification.